I0465077

By Author and Illustrator: Joseph Sumpter

Book Title: Adult Coloring Book: Lovely Owls Designs For Stress Relief and Relaxation

Beautiful and lovely owls for adults to enjoy coloring for stress reduction and relaxation coloring beautiful owls.

Biography

Joseph Sumpter enjoys sports, traveling, creating books, and working.

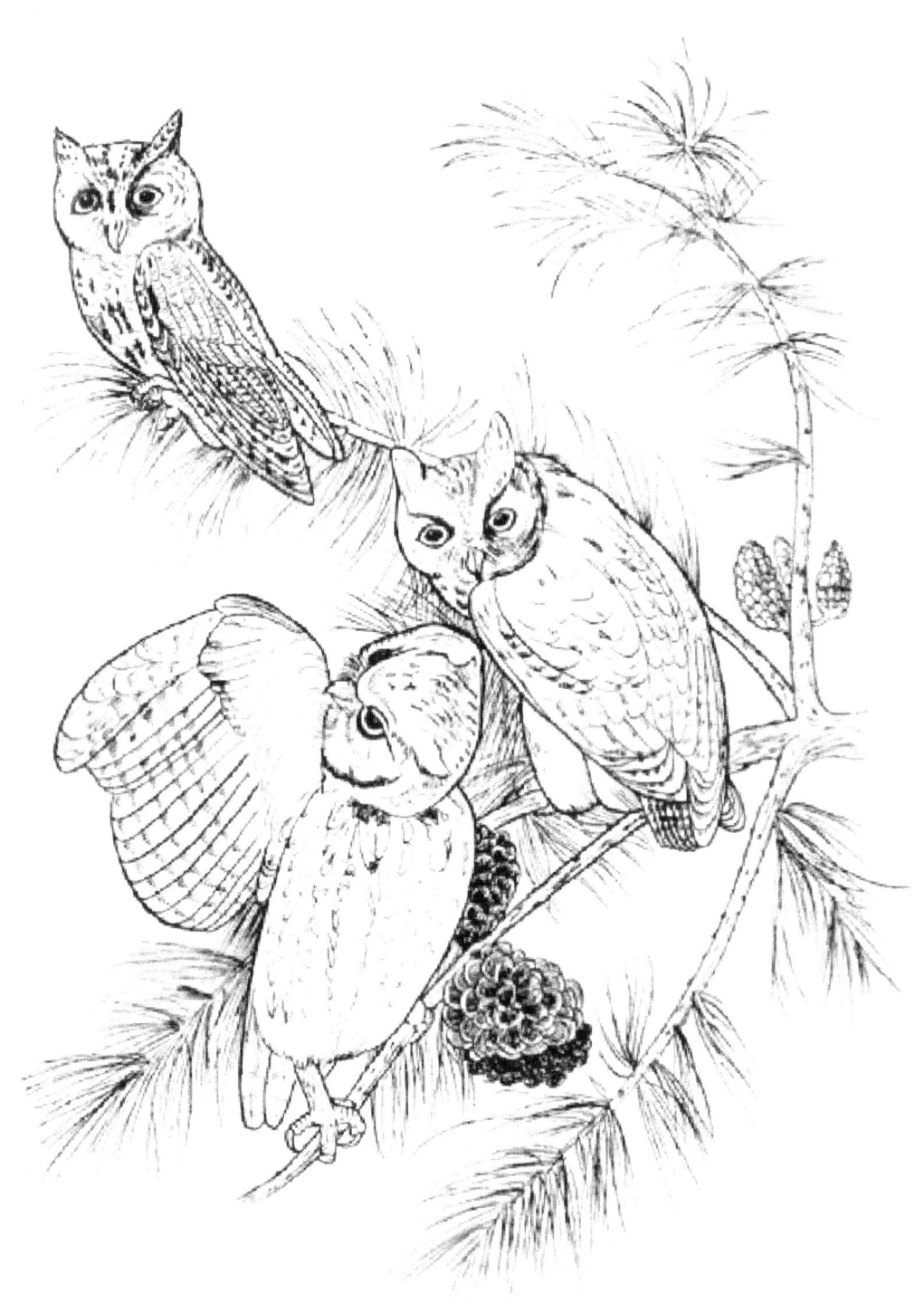

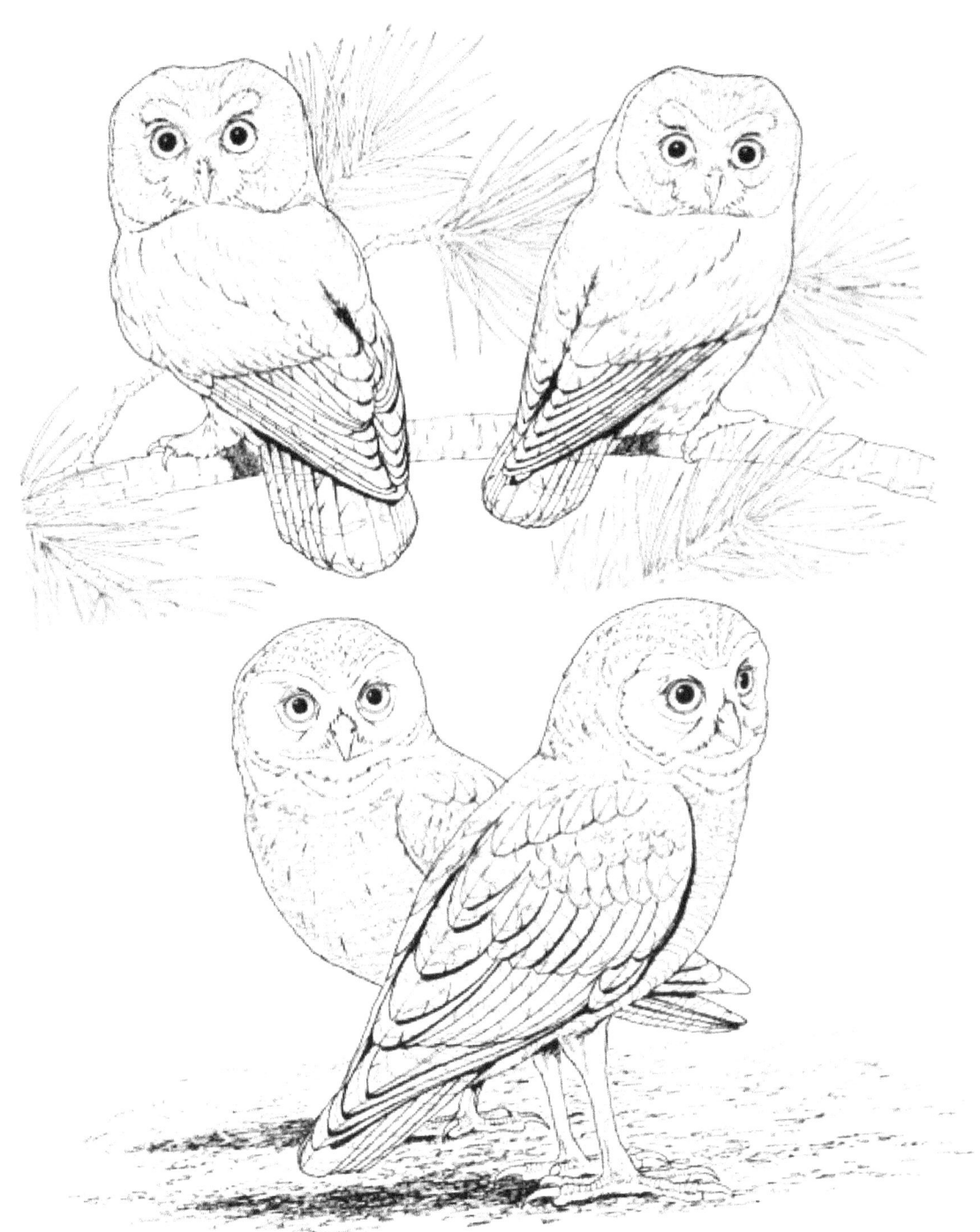

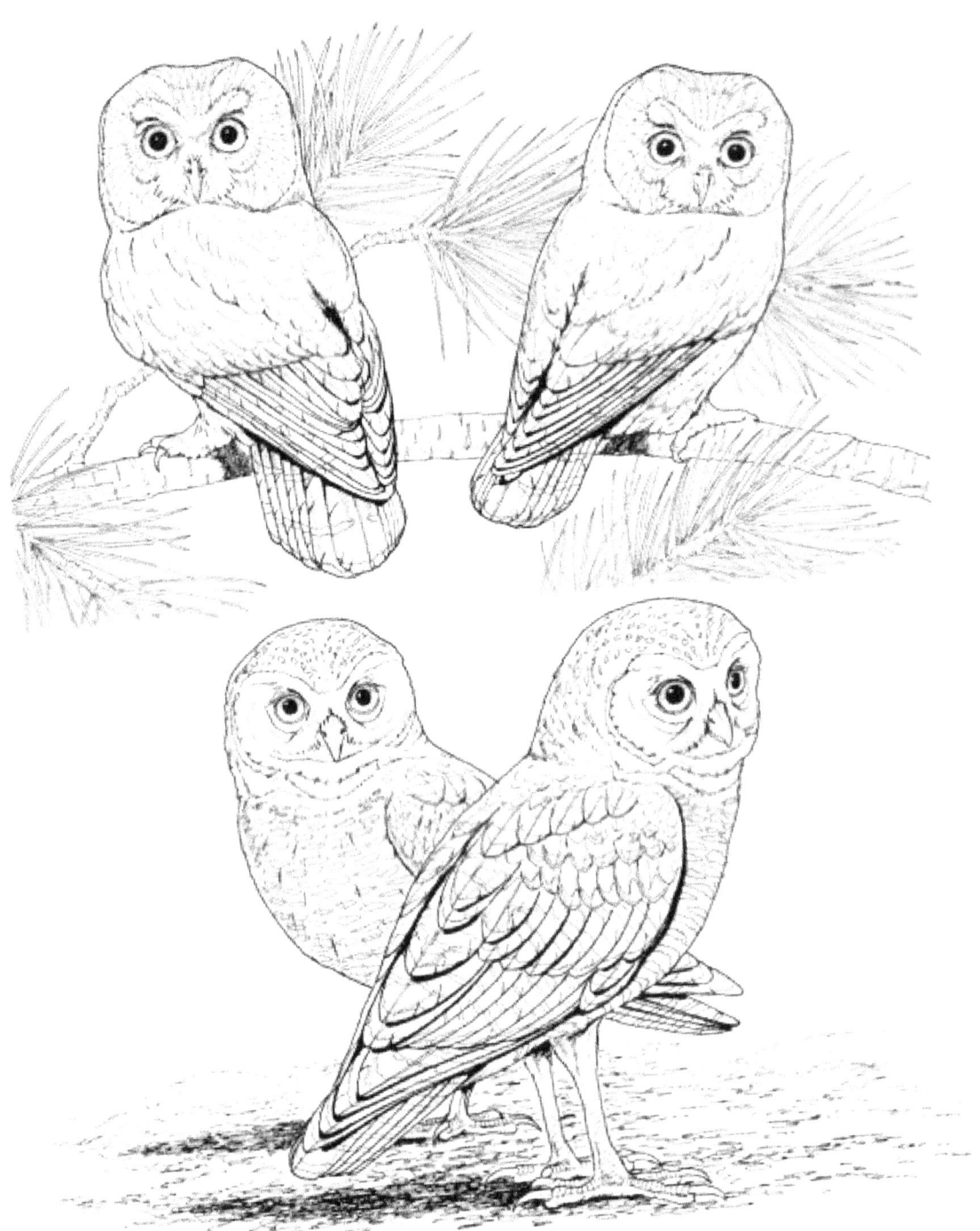

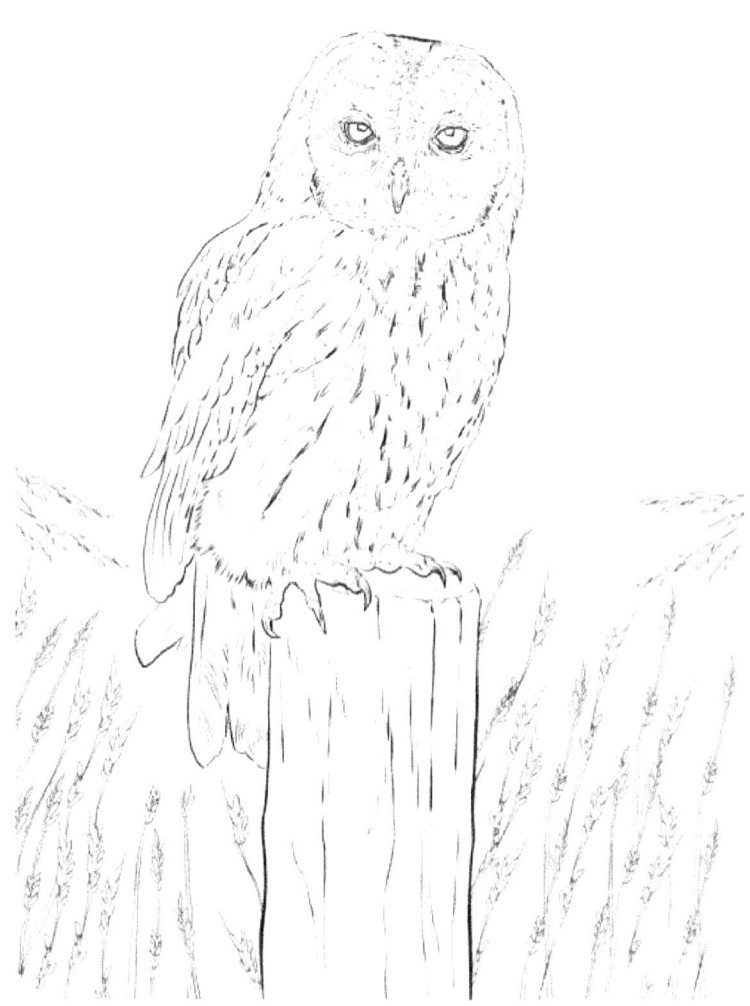

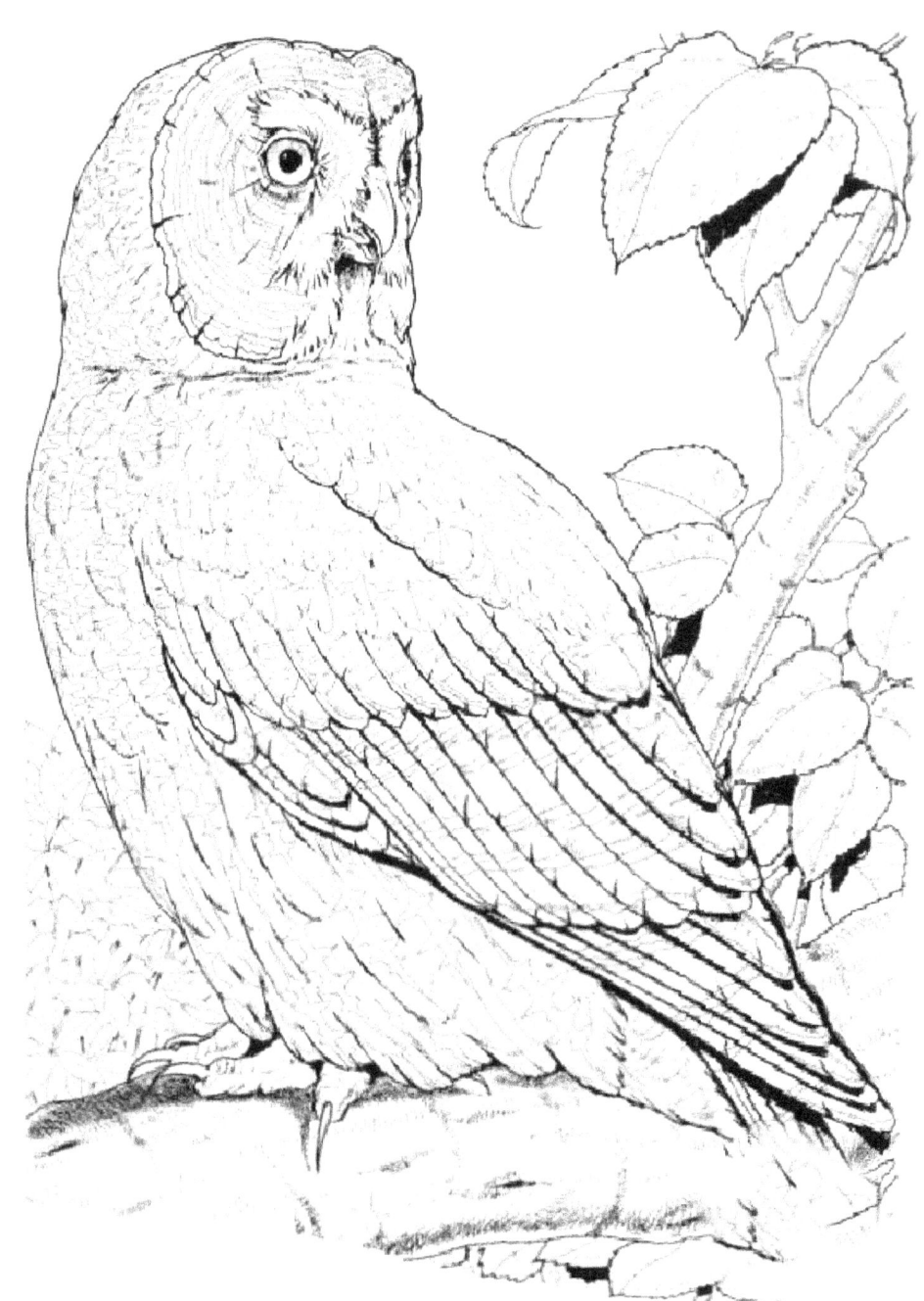

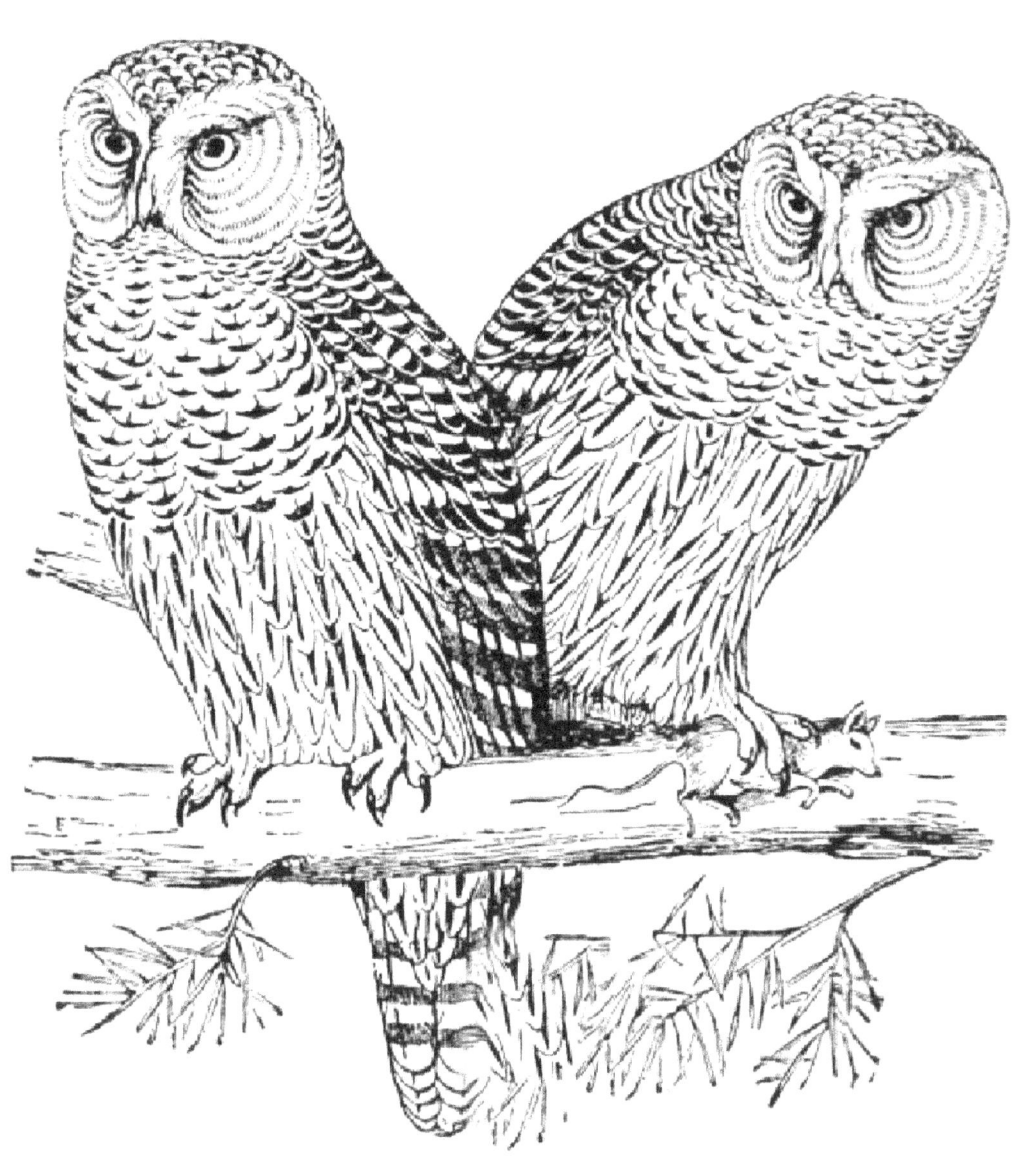

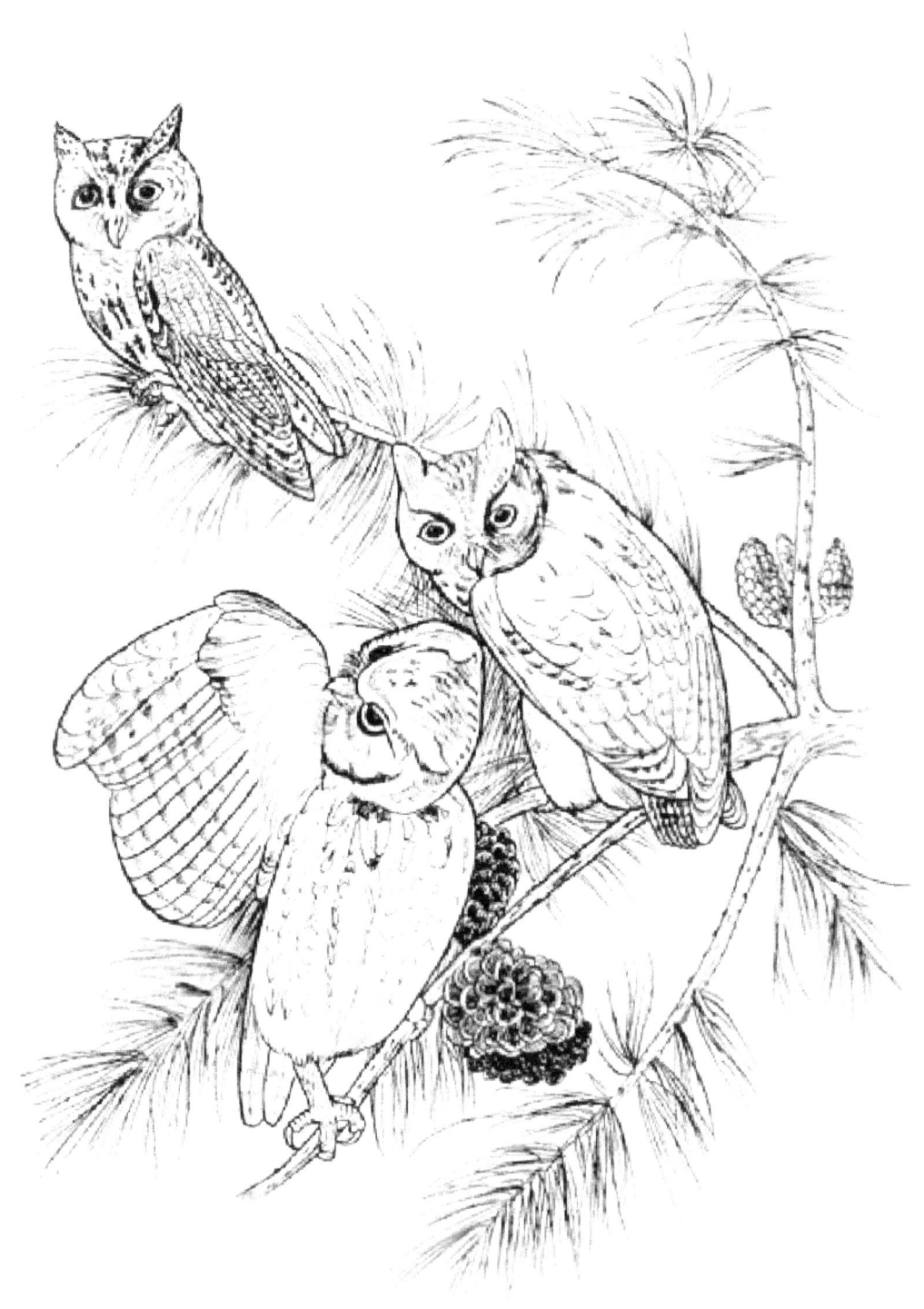

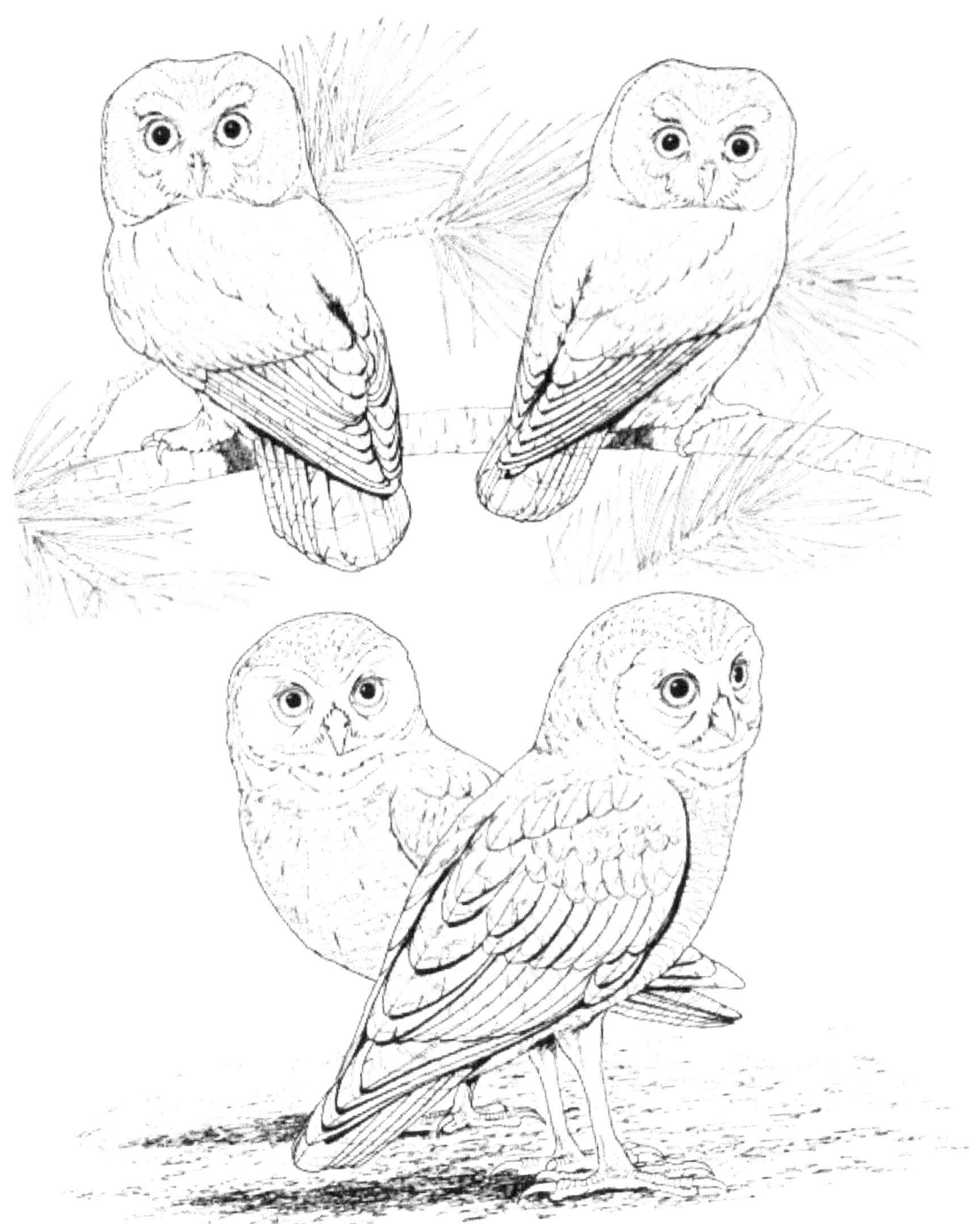

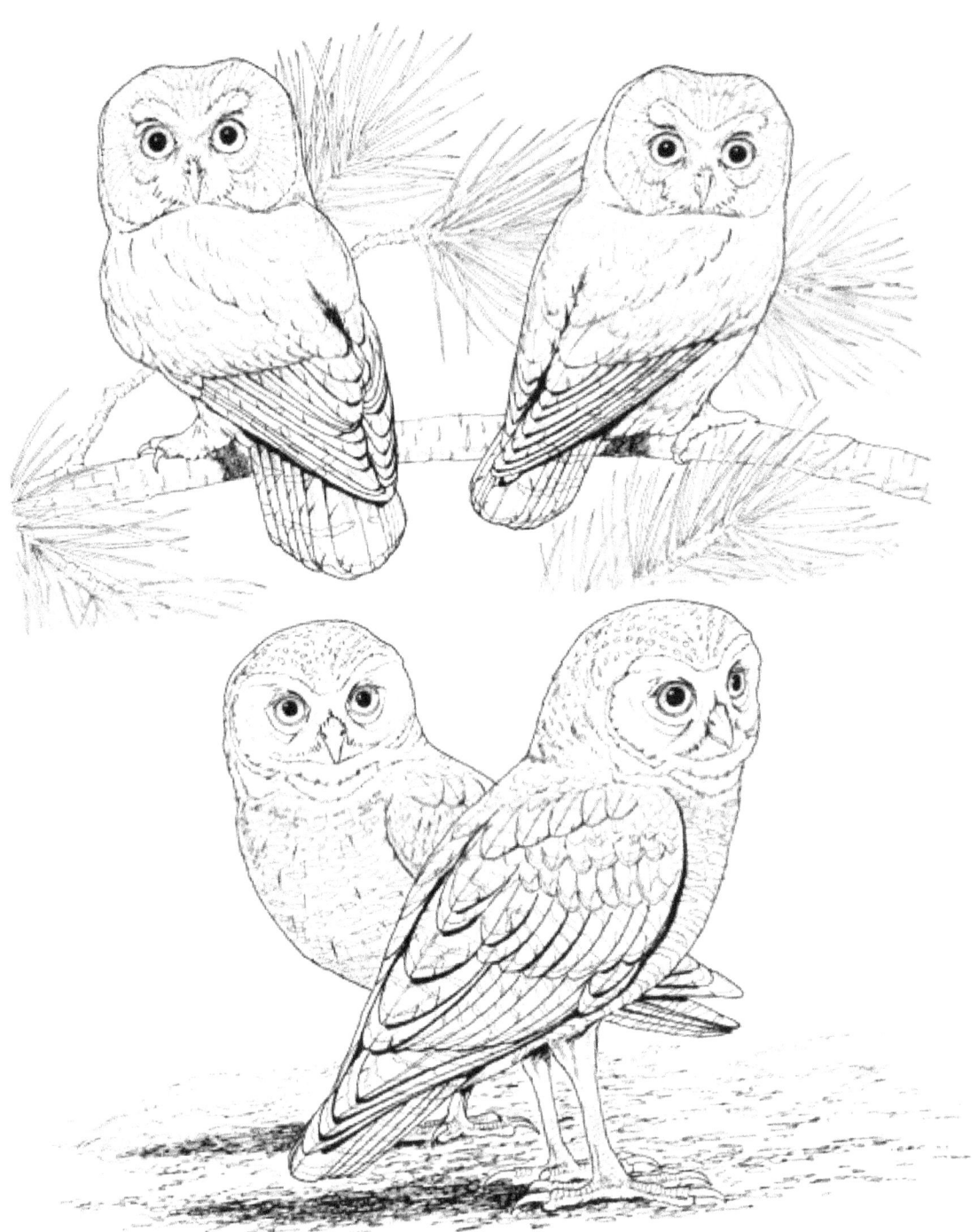

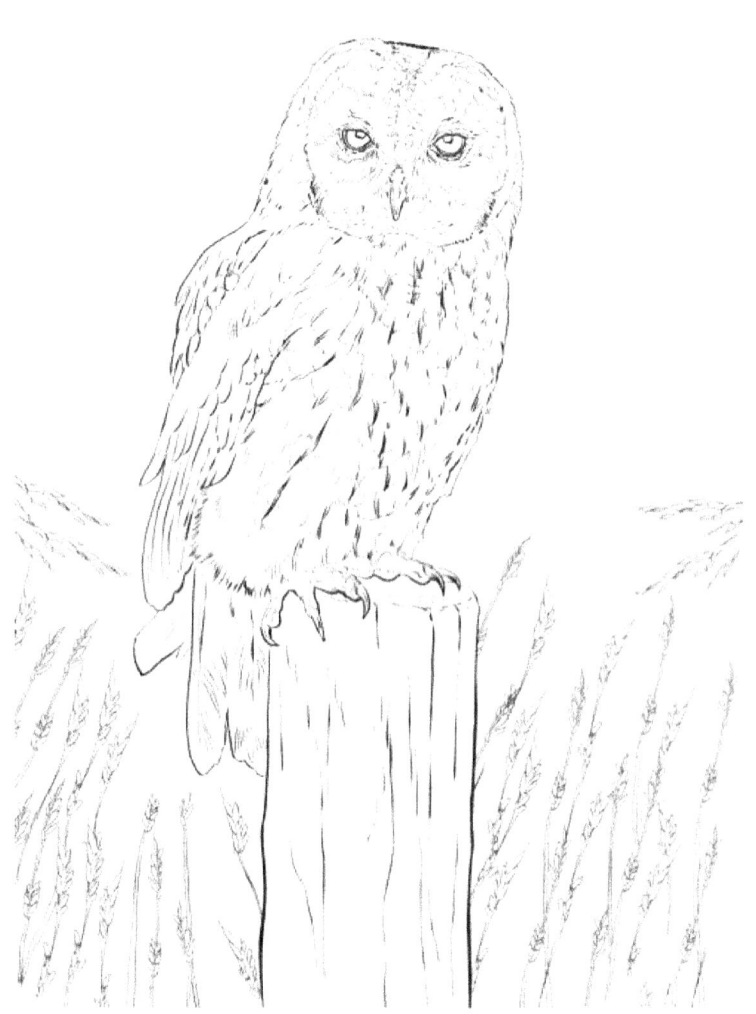

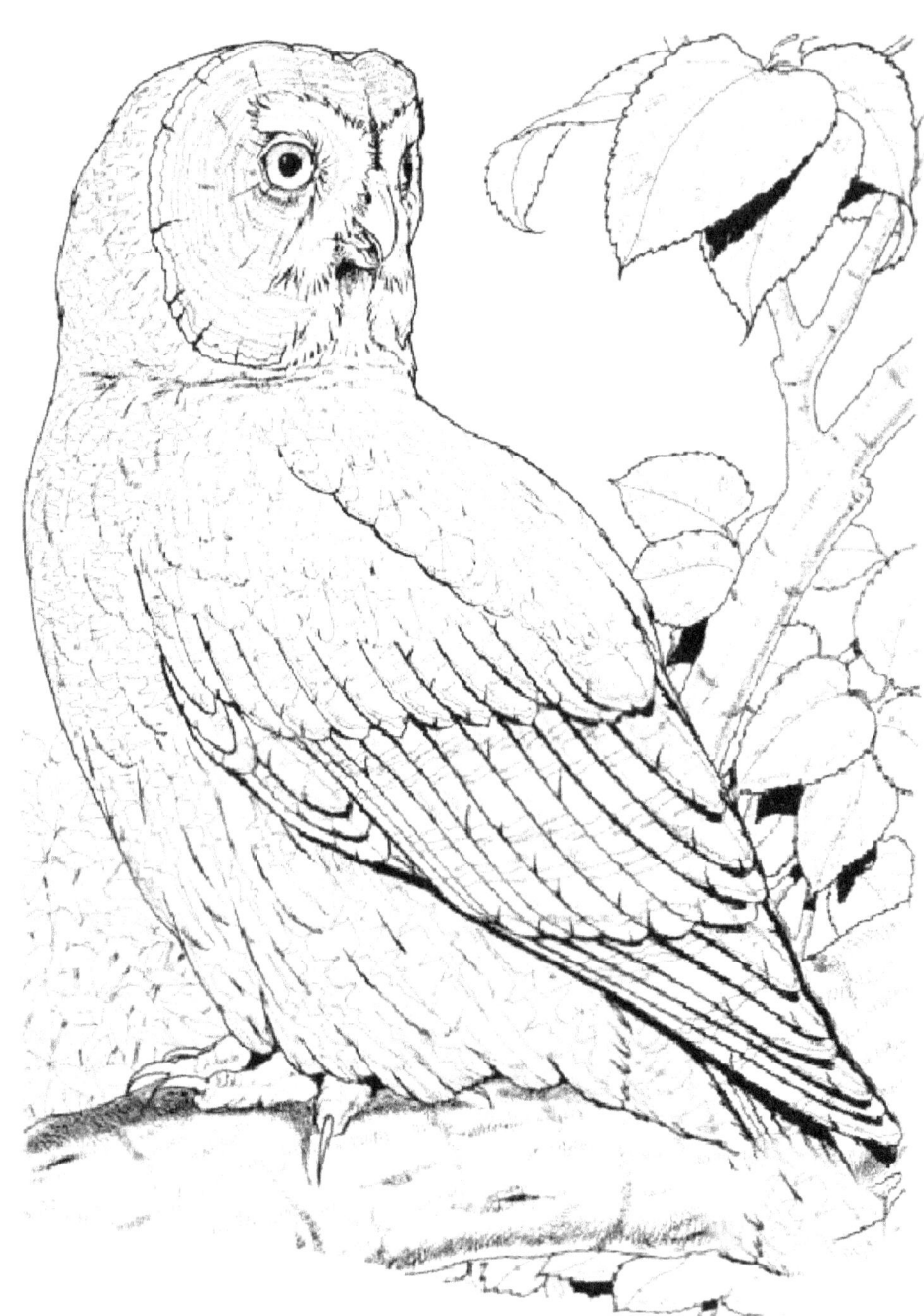

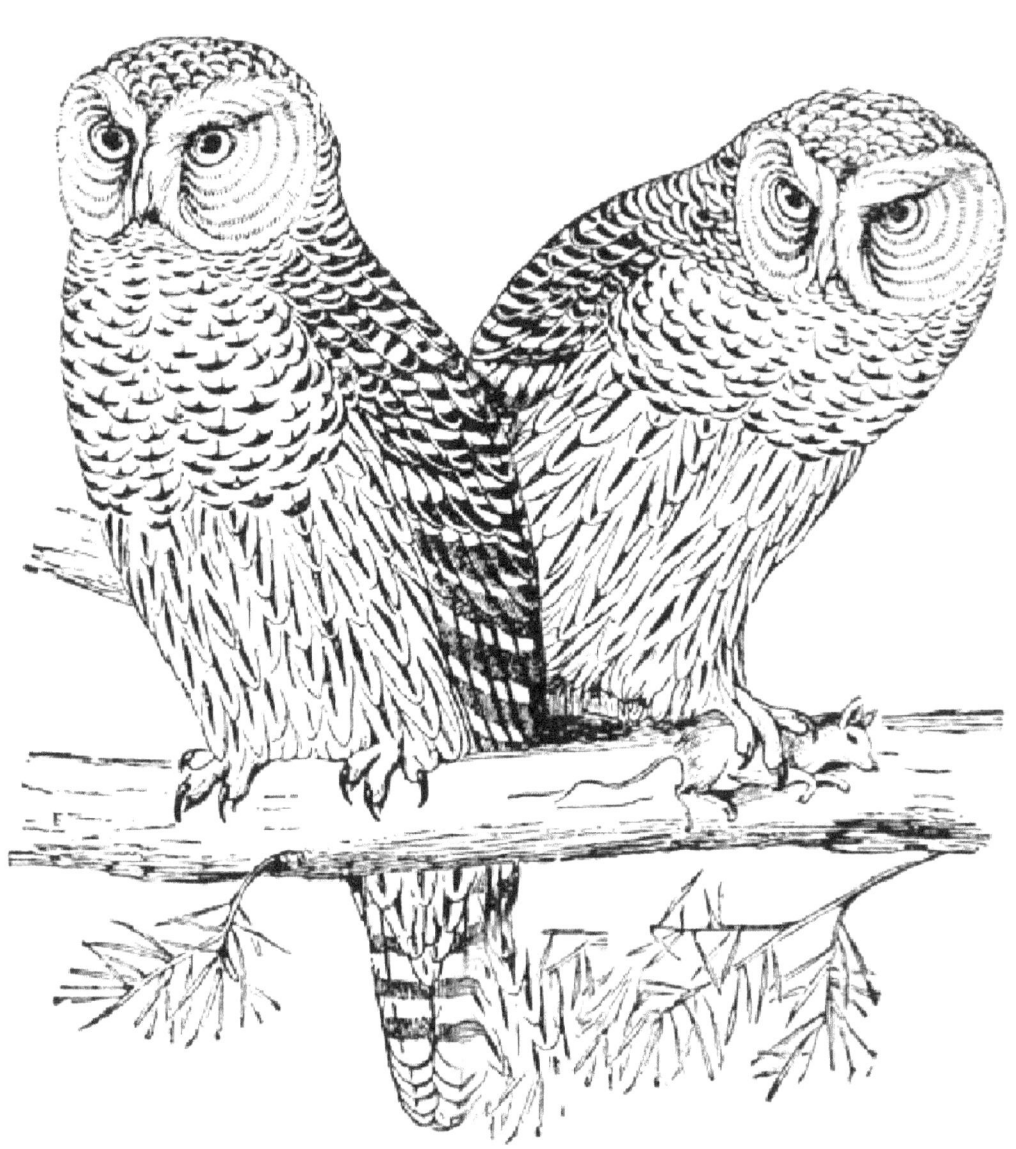

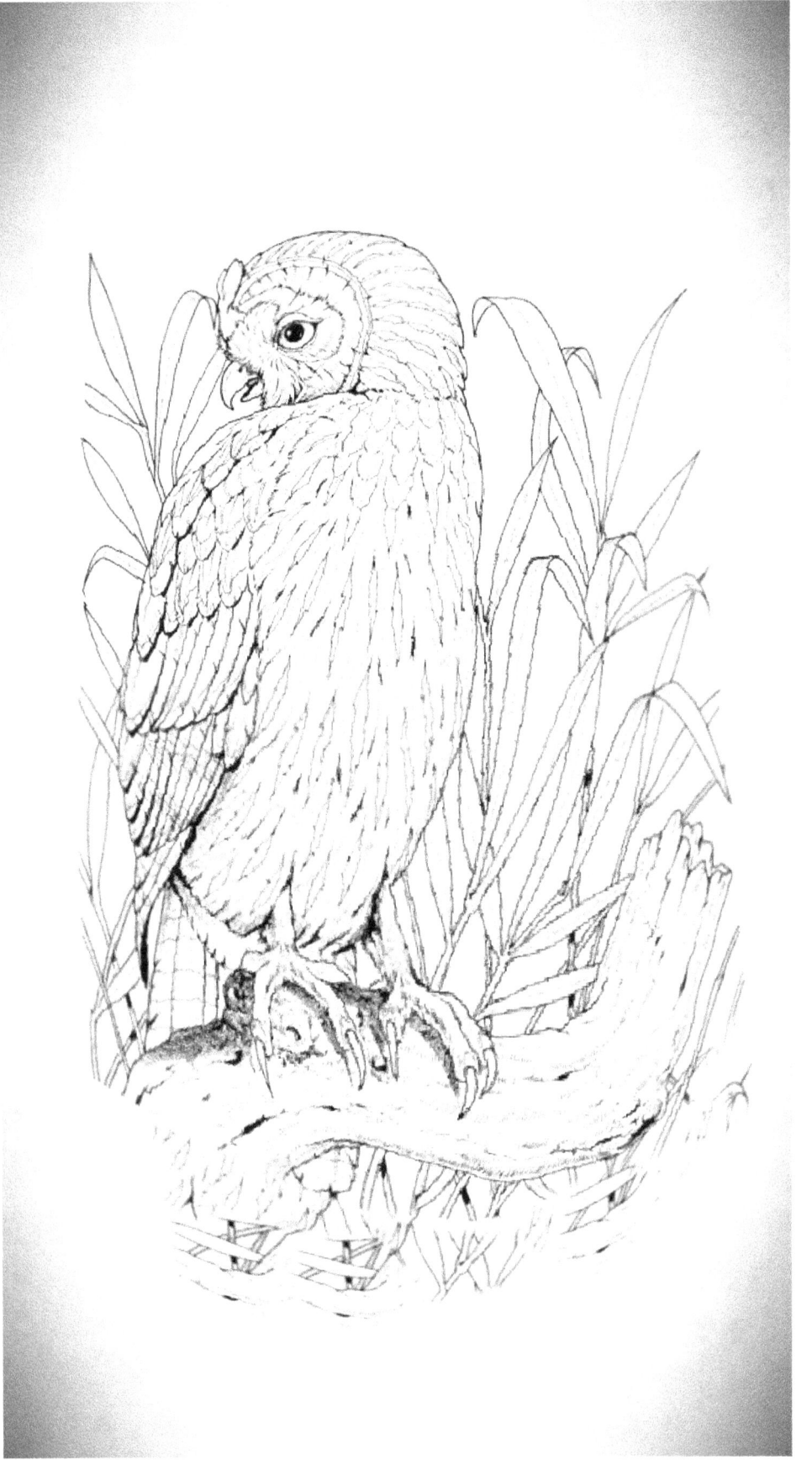

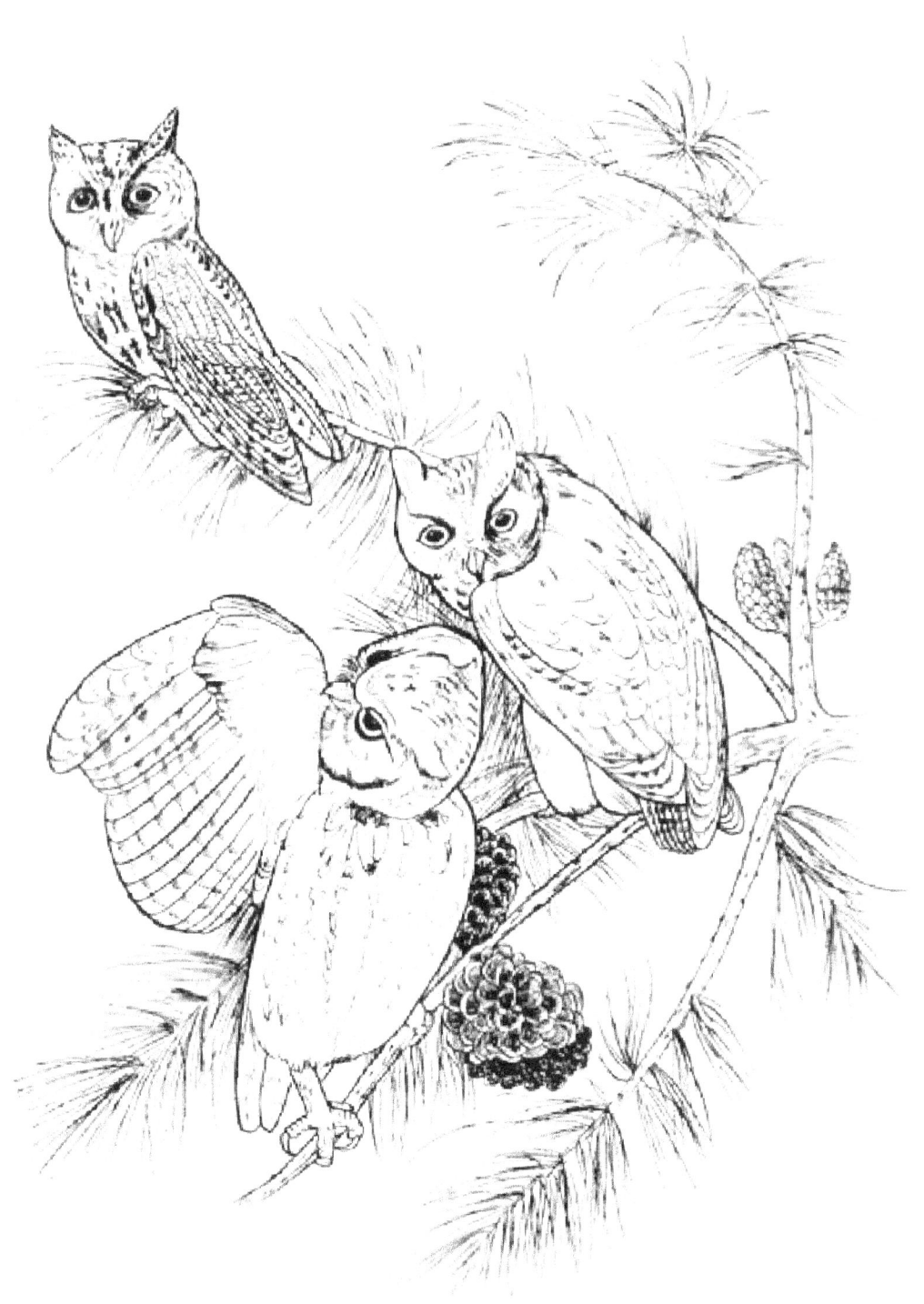

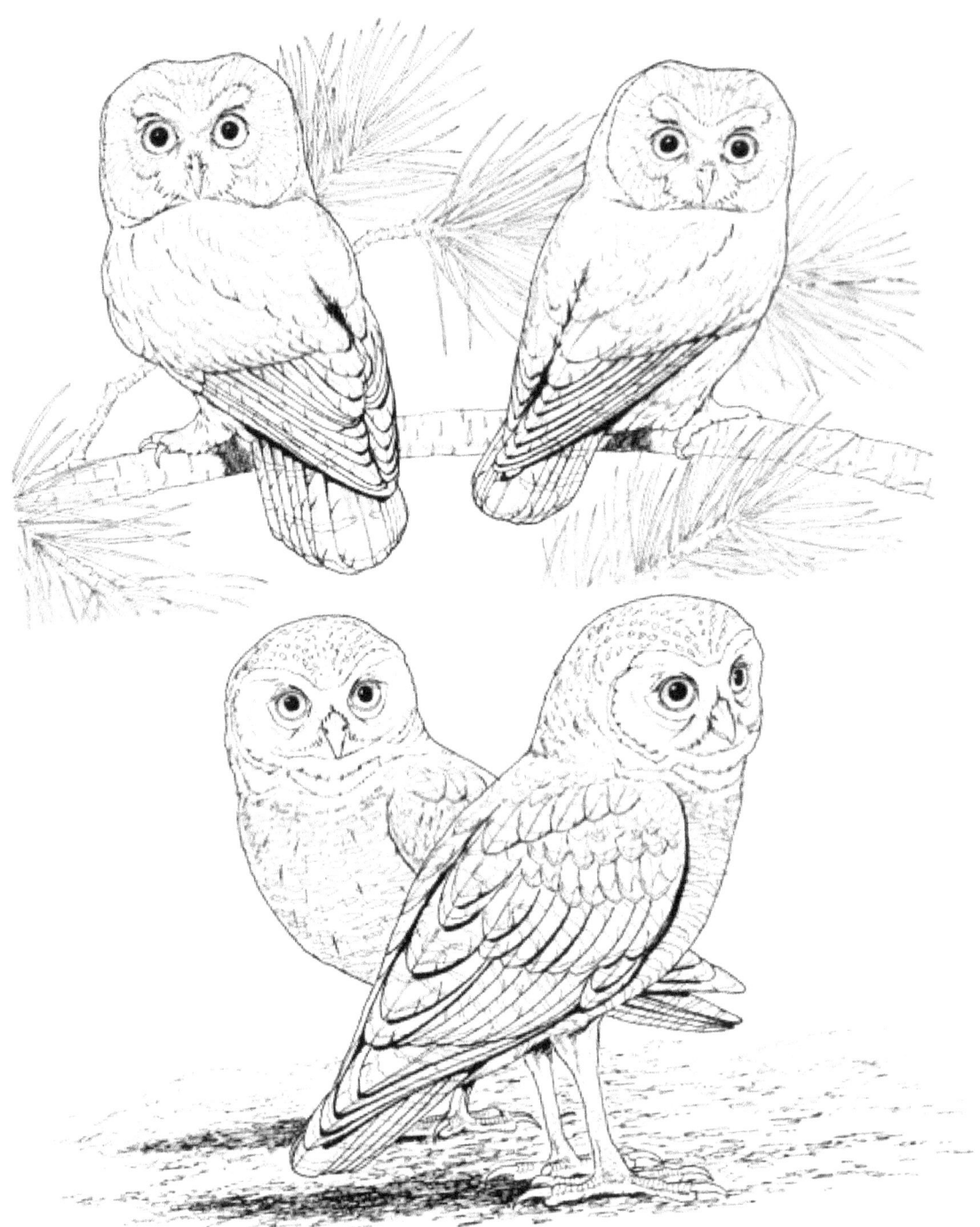

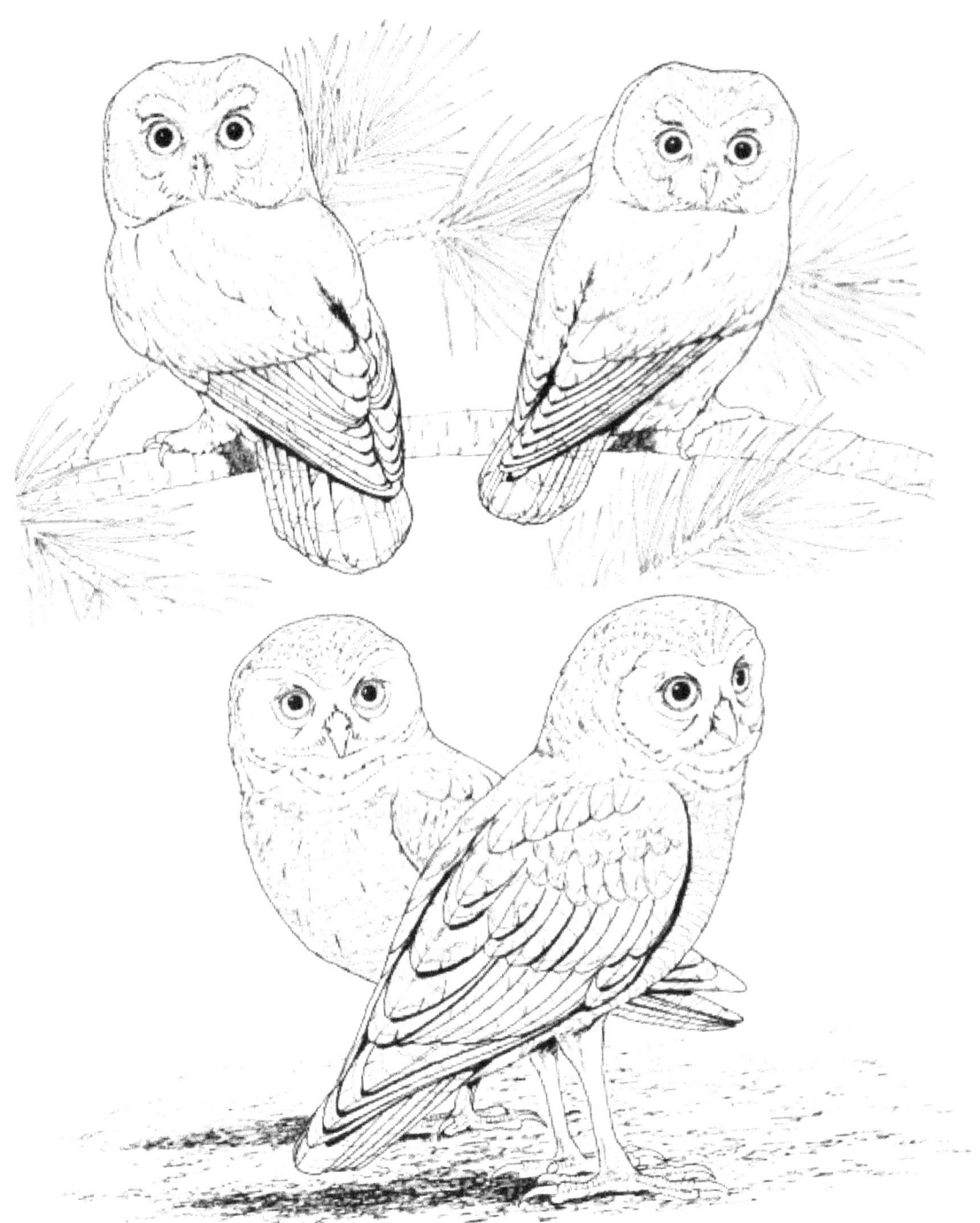

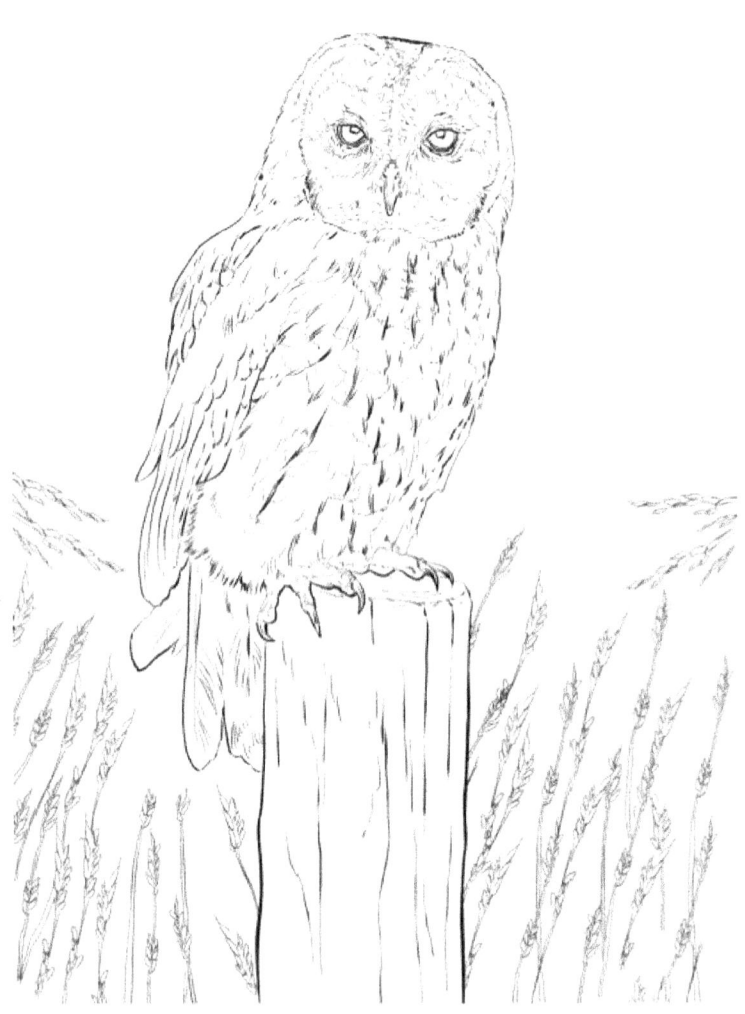

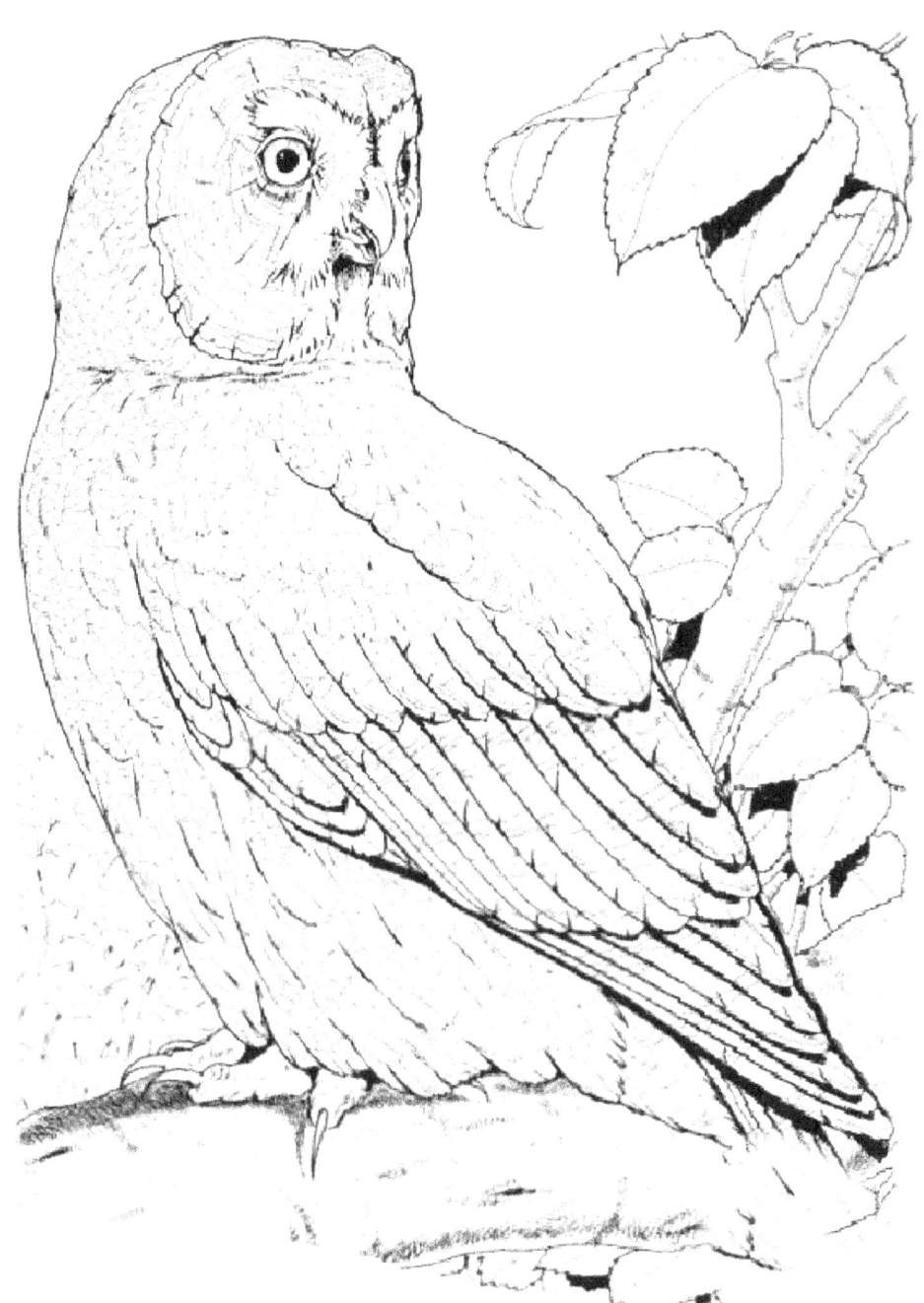

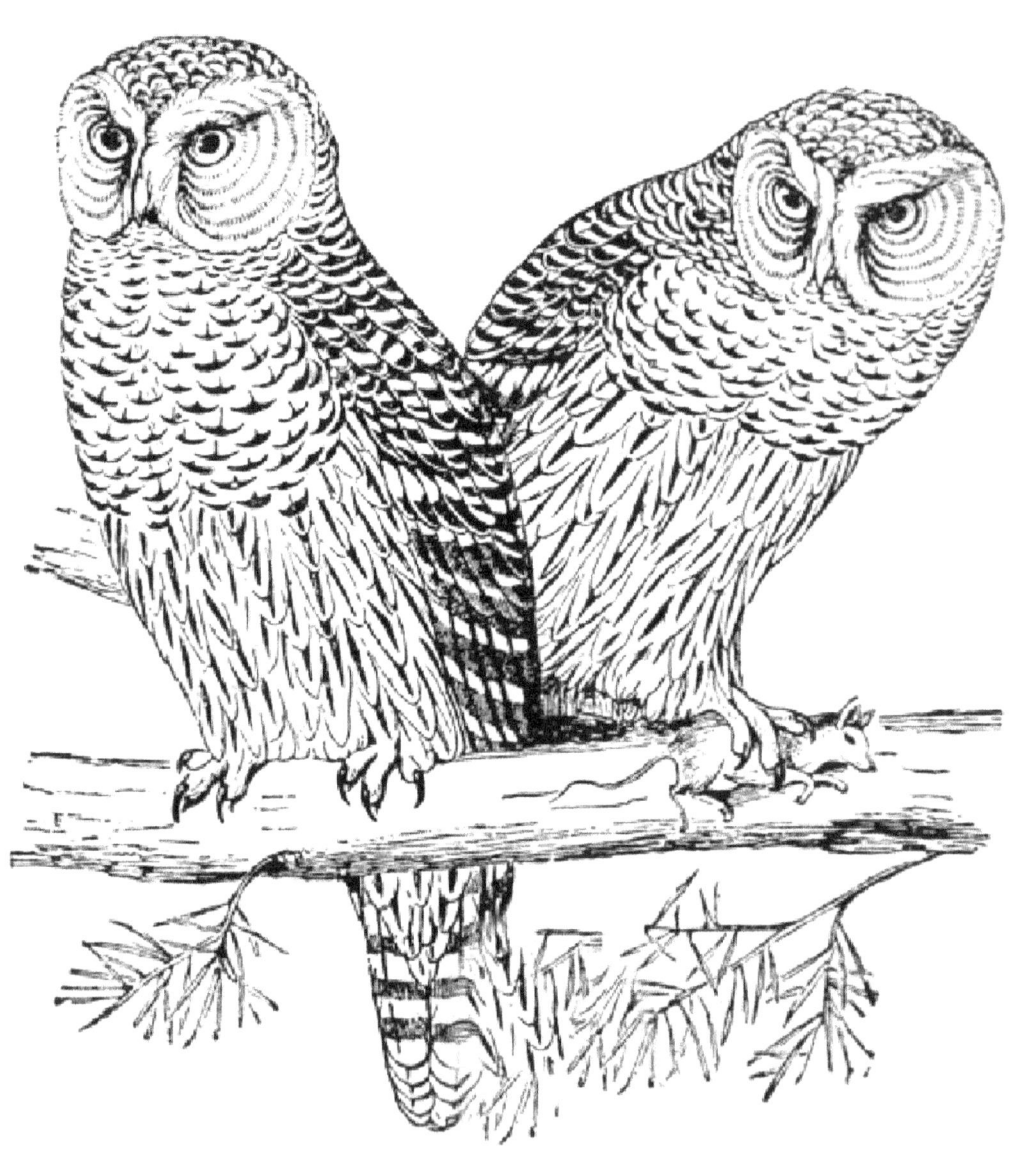

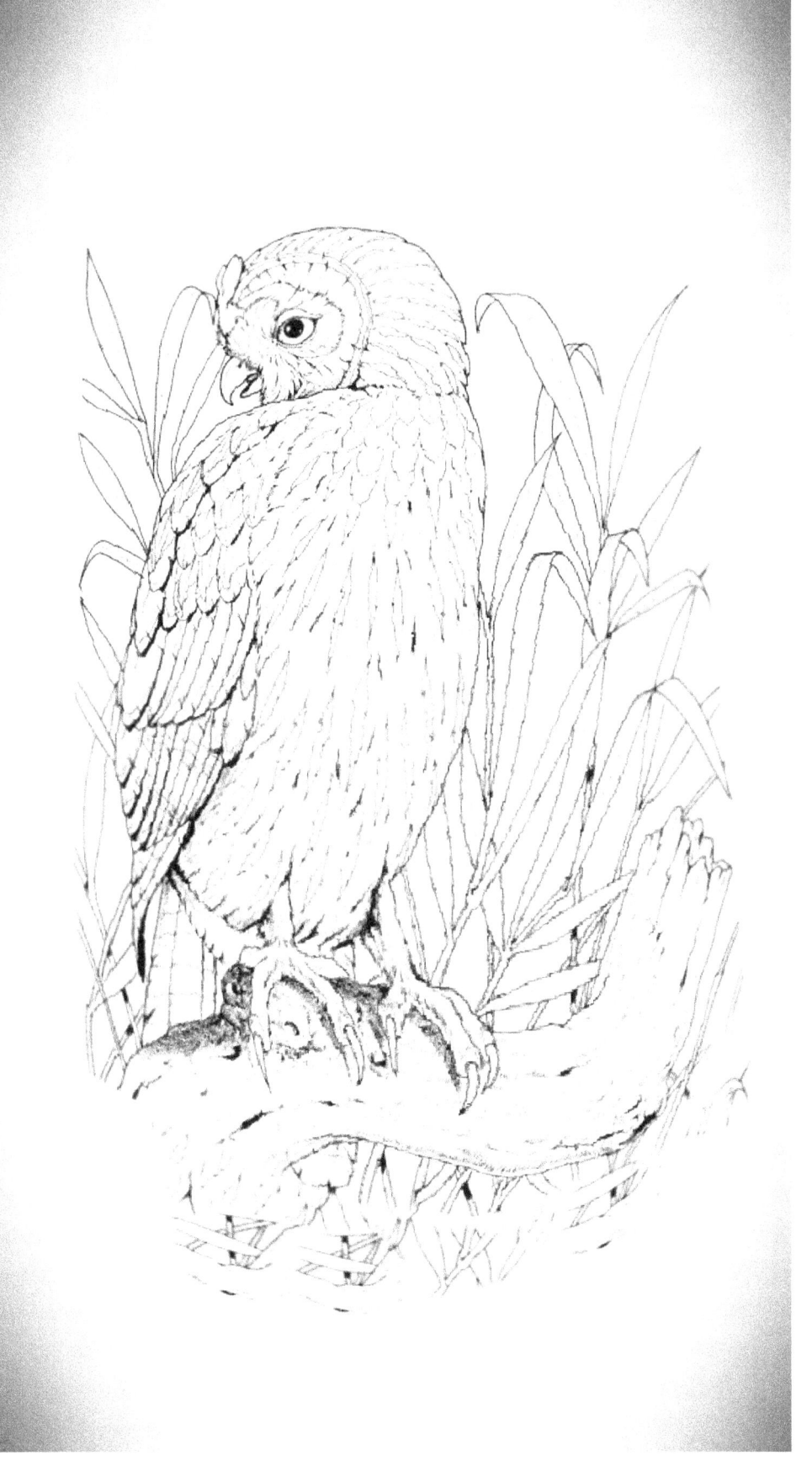

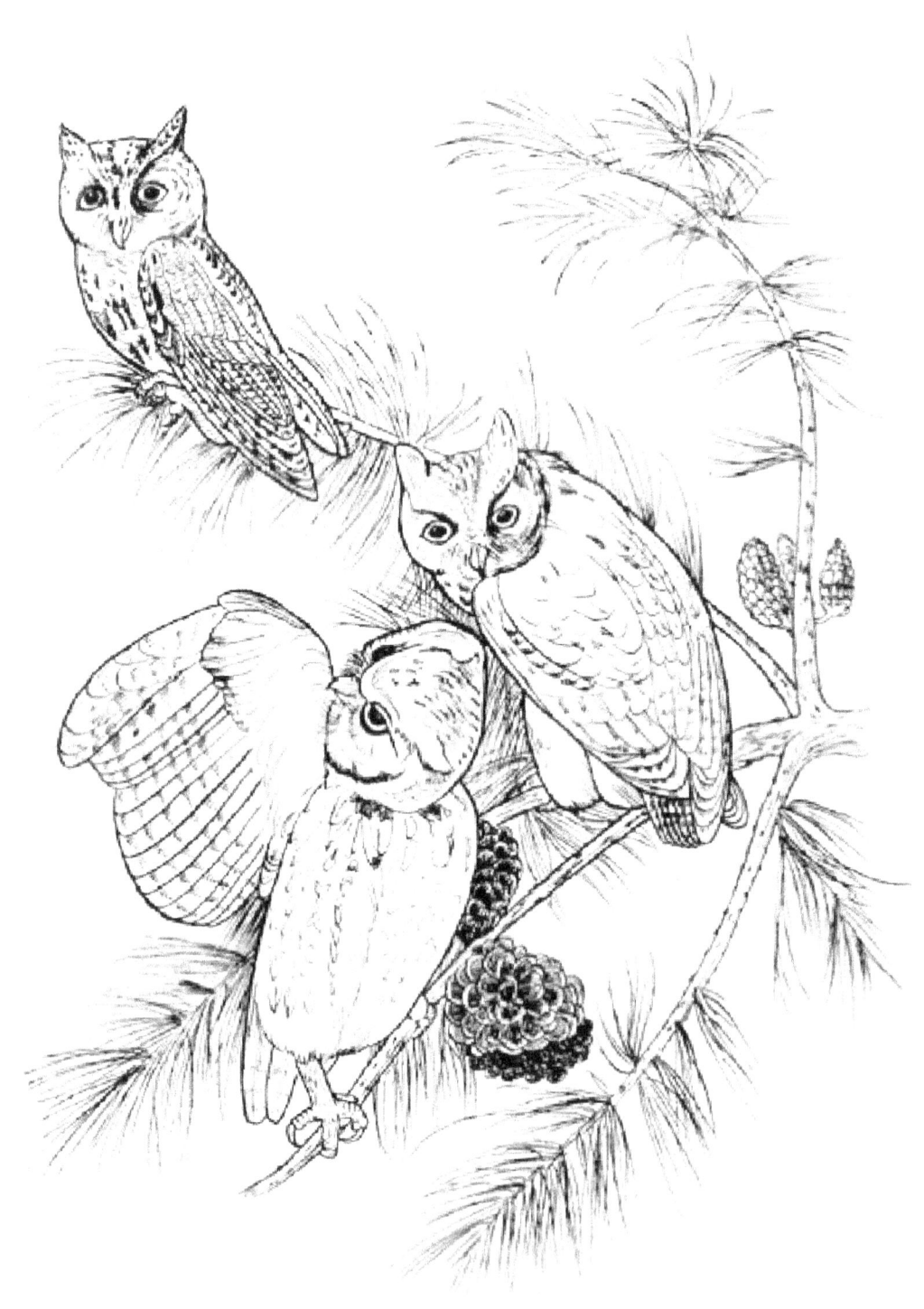

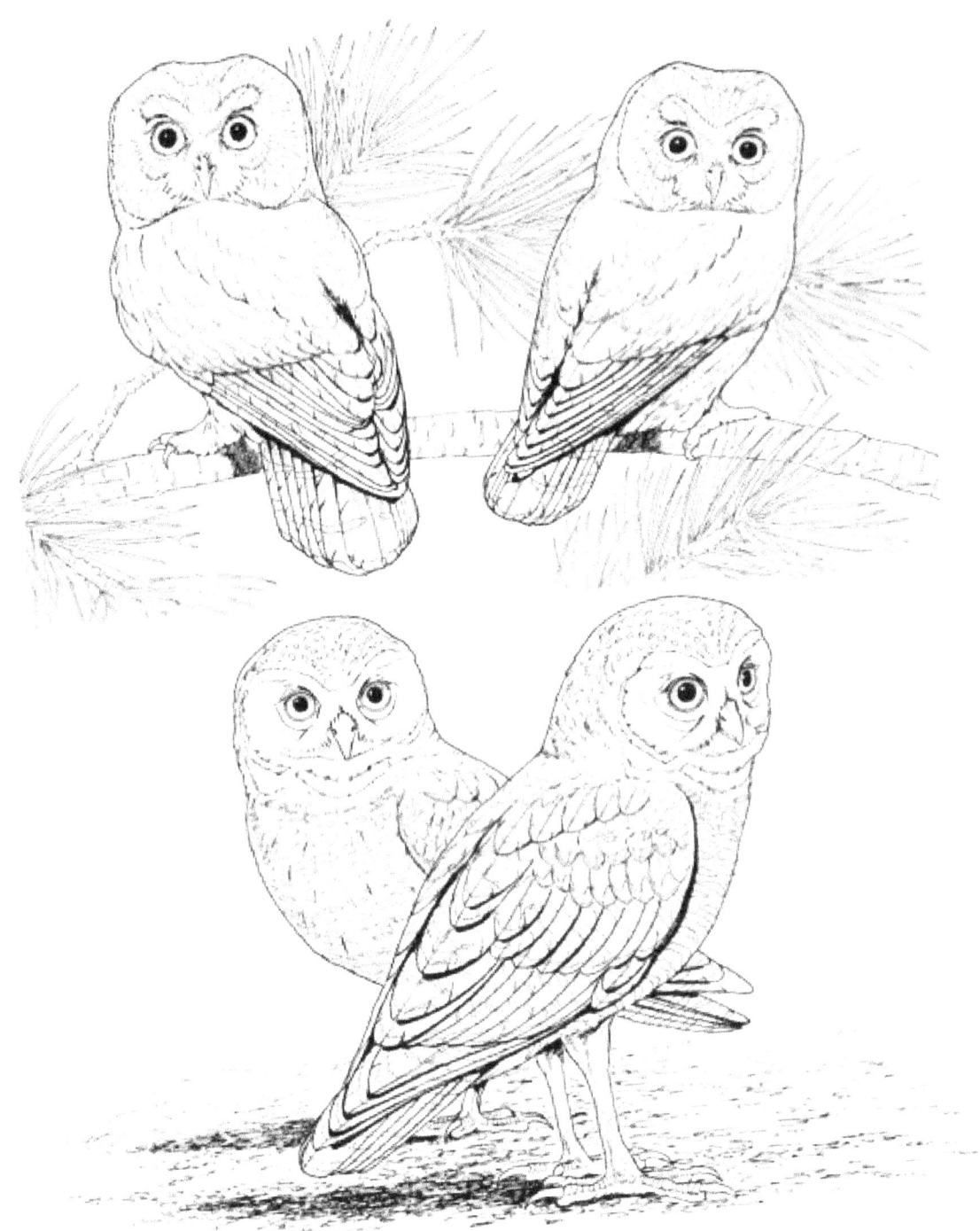

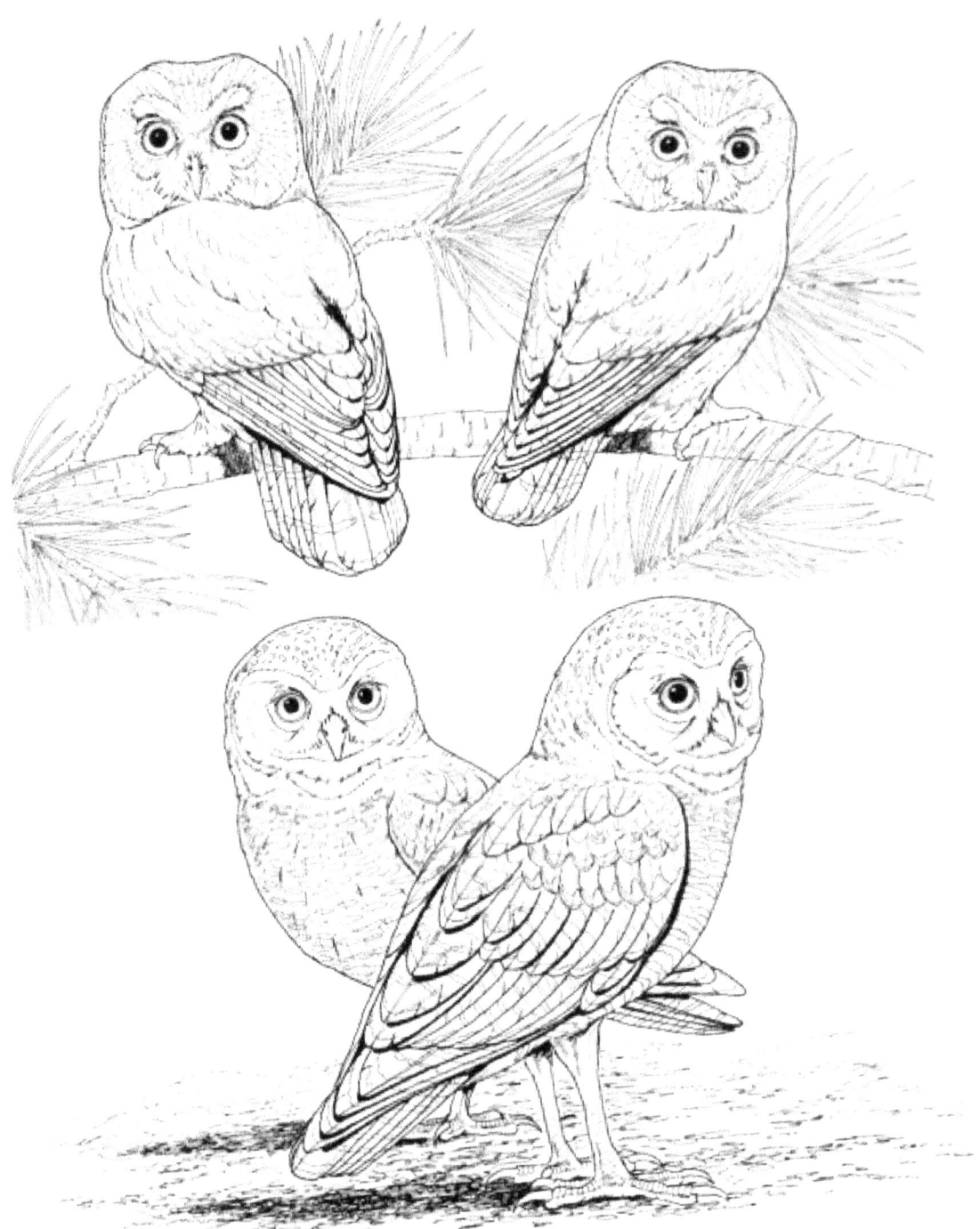

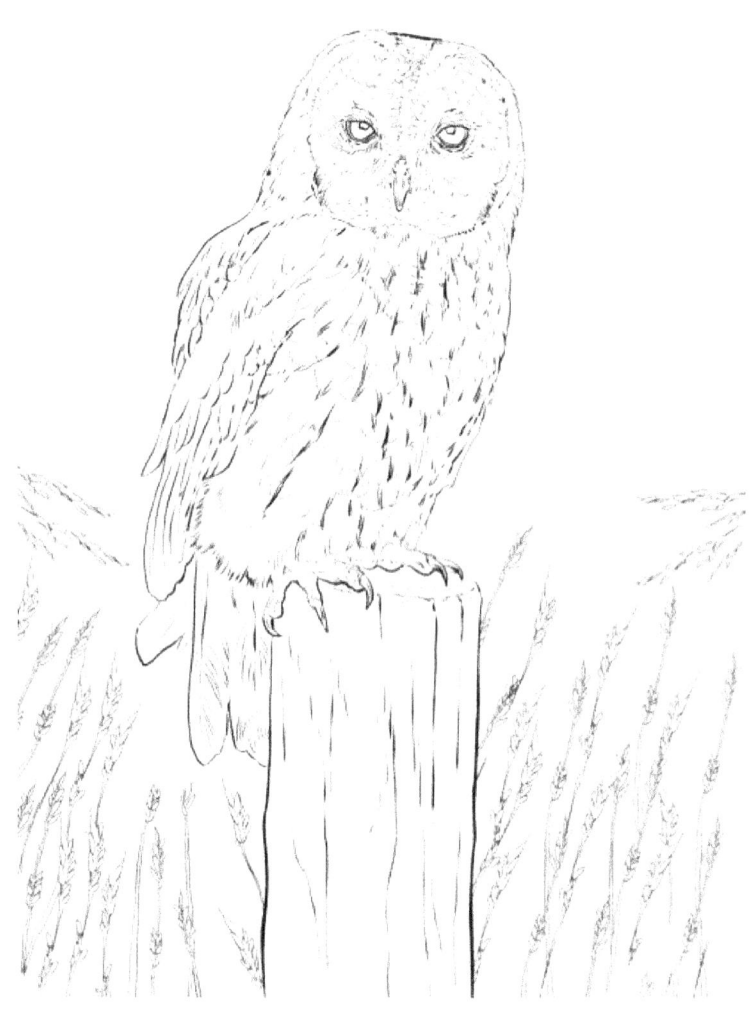

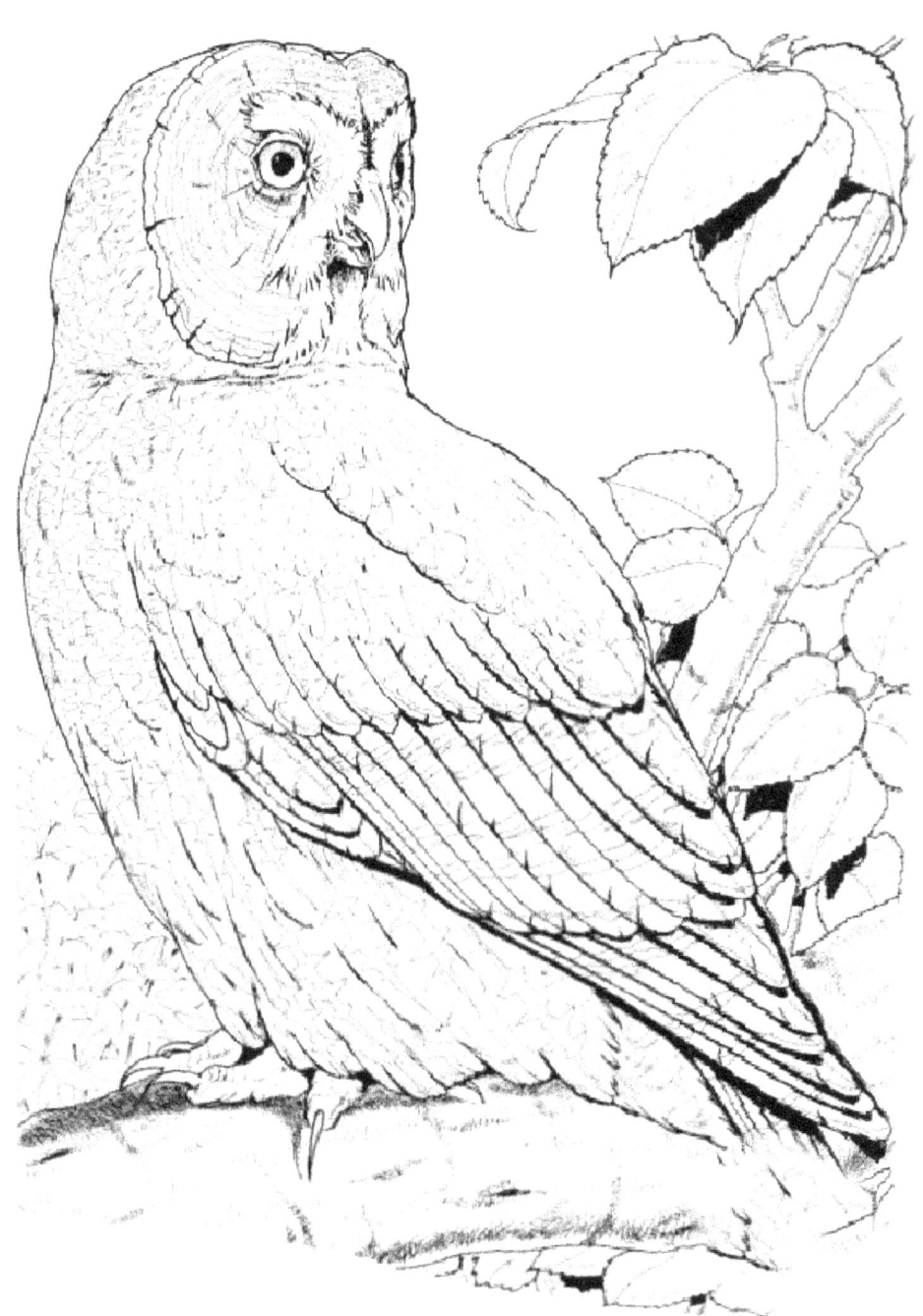

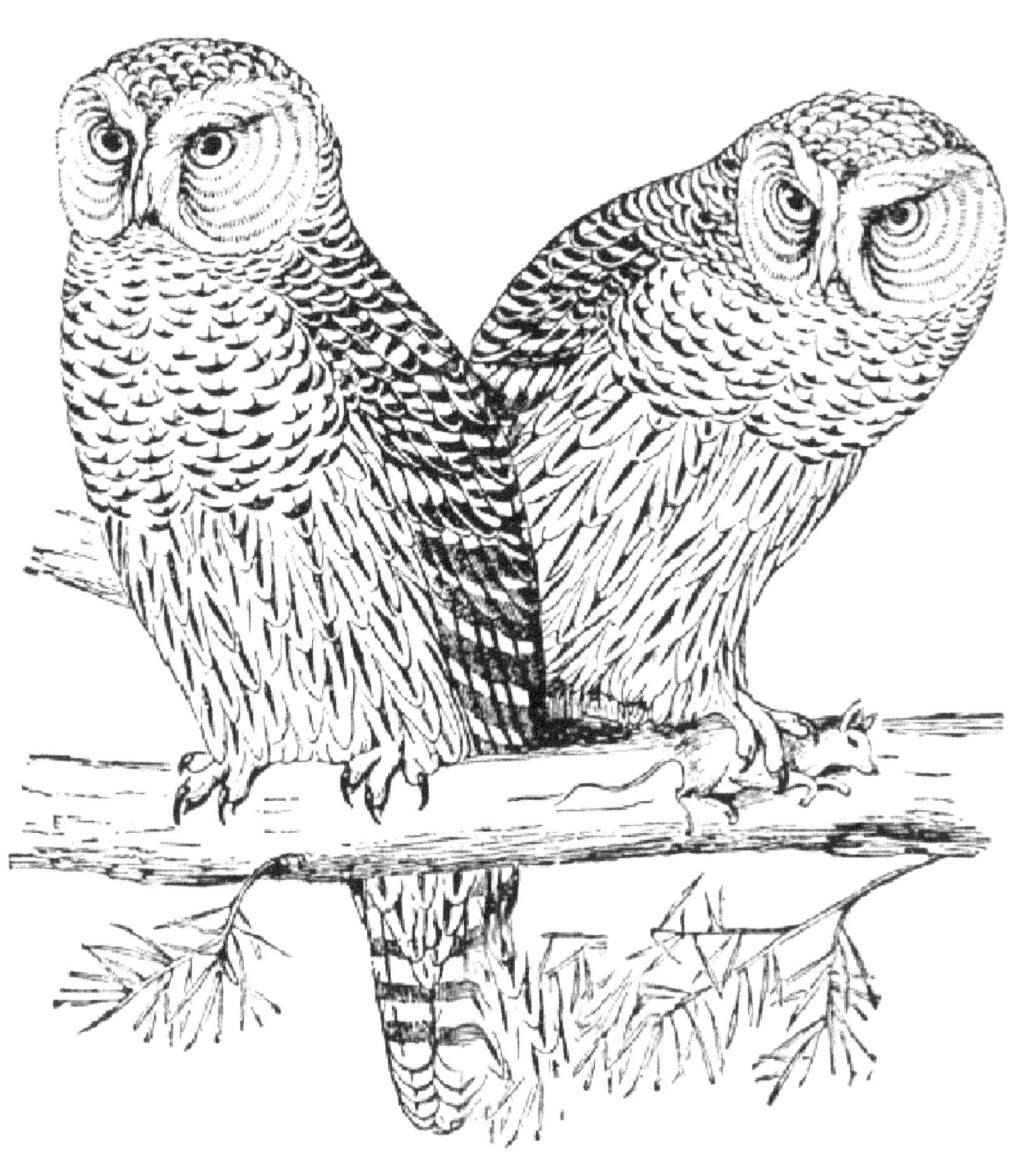

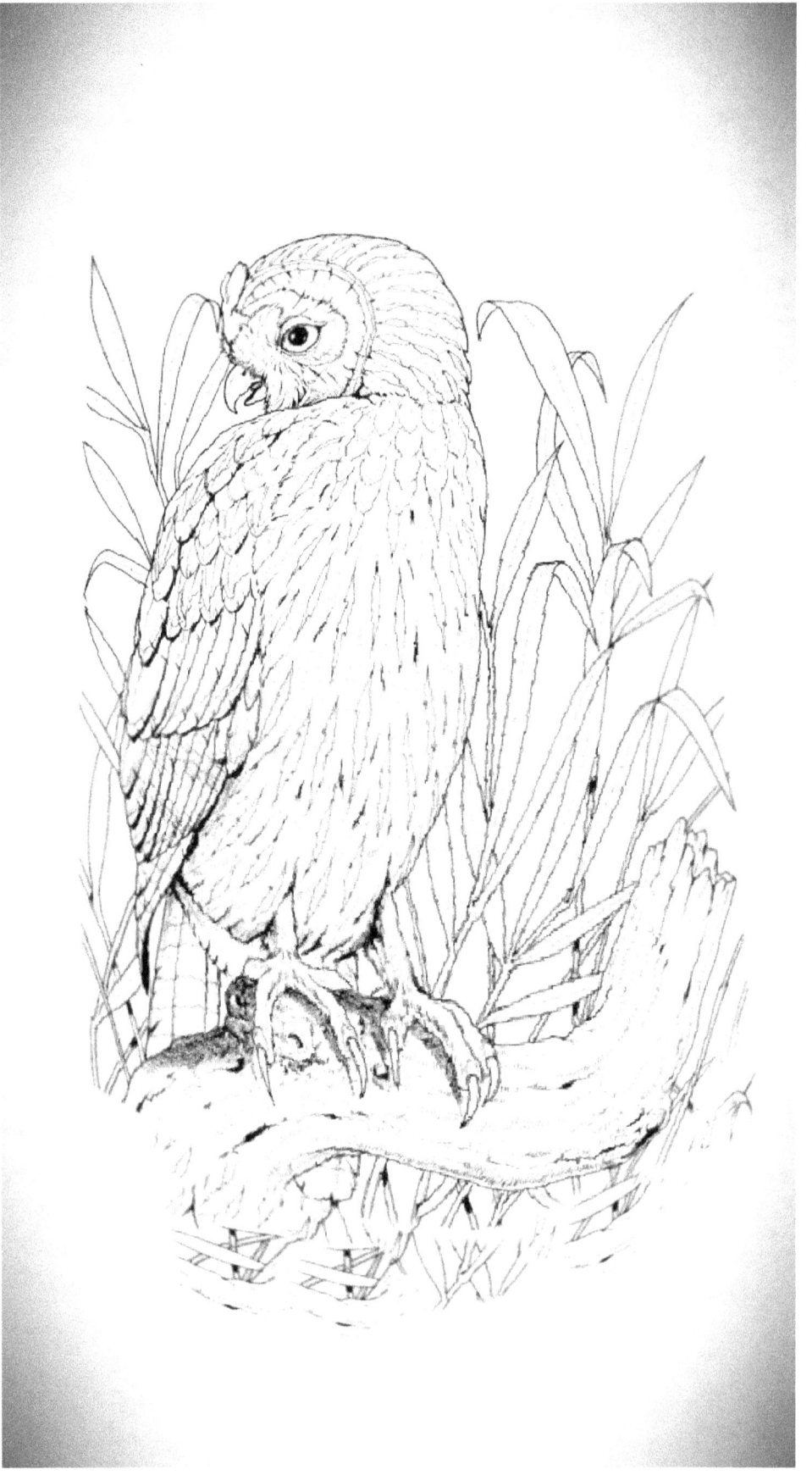

www.ingramcontent.com/pod-product-compliance
Lightning Source LLC
Chambersburg PA
CBHW081317180526
45170CB00007B/2749